Accepting the Call

BY

Minister Kevin B. Thomas

Accepting the Call

Min.Kevin B.Thomas
P.O. Box 541
Belleville, Michigan 48112

ISBN-978-1-60458-545-2
Publisher InstantPublisher-Knd Enterprise
Printed in the United States of America
©2009 By Min.Kevin B. Thomas
All rights reserved. No part of this book shall be reproduced, stored in a retrieval system, or transmitted by any means without written permission from the author.

Bibliography

Scripture references from King James some I paraphrased and the Bible Knowledge Commentary [1]Merriam-Webster, I. (2003). *Merriam-Webster's collegiate dictionary.* Includes index. (Eleventh ed.). Springfield, Mass.: Merriam-Webster, Inc.

Dedication

To my wife and children my family and friends I thank you for your support and love. To my Mt. Zion Church family and fellow ministerial staff thank you all. To the wonderful new beginnings class for the past two years and my co-teacher Rev. Joe Stephens thanks for allowing me to present to you what God has been sharing with me. Thank you all for your Prayers. And thank you for accepting the Call.

Accepting the Call

BY

Minister Kevin B. Thomas

Table of Contents

Foreword 7

Preface 9

Introduction 10

Chapters

1. Call for a People 13

2. The Devil Made My Bed and I Slept In It 20

3. Unity by Design ...…..26

4. A Prayer for God's Pardon for Self 33

5. Why do bad things happen to Good People? 40

6. Dying for a Man 47

7. The Call of a Deliver, Don't Move Until God Says move 50

Foreword

Man's predestined life, the life God has chosen and planned for his called out one's is living with the abundance of God's Power, Love and the benefits of his Grace and Mercy. Accepting the call means walking in God's true authority. This book is just a sample and example of how to live, worship and have the blessings of God upon your life and experience the very presence of God while being in the center of his will. God's road map of Life is clear to some and others may need a guide to help conquer the challenges of today's modern world and to recognize the many devices of the enemy. Having a clear understanding of who we are as the people of God the body of Christ, and most importantly who you are as a person is vital to the success of the walk we have in Christ. Born in sin all coming short of his Glory, being bought by a price the price of death by Jesus Christ which we receive to brings us to repentance into salvation, setting us on a clear and narrow path of righteousness to fulfill our true destiny. Knowing that the call is yours, whose call will you accept? May Gods blessings and

Peace be upon you as you accept his call on Your Life?

Sid C. Frye

President of the Music Dept. District #11 COGIC/President of Soul Investment

Preface

Accepting the call is about the many things that are faced by beleivers, things that has cause many to walk away or even protend by just going through the motions of Church. The battles that will be faced are from loved ones, friends, and even spouses and children, the most dangerous and hardest to conquer are the battles in ones own mind. Accepting the call means more than just being saved it's submitting your will to God and being able to submit to the Man or Women of God he has sat you under. The real deal is renewing your mind to the word God and putting that word known into action, staying consistant in prayer and study and dying to self.

Introduction

The thought of coming up on the rough side of the mountain is a human and carnal way to try to fix sin that people are still feeling condemned about. This type of attitude makes you feel you have to do something to make it into the family of God. When you are called into a thing whether it's a game, a meeting, a club or even a party the person that has called you is not asking you to bring anything, change anything or buy anything they are just saying come. For anyone to call or invite you to something is a priviledge and an honor and to accept the call is to agree that the caller has everything you need to enjoy and do that which he is calling you to do. We have to start being the word of God alive, throughout the Bible the people of God that trusted him walked in victory all the time not because they were great but because the one they trusted in is great. Scripture has taught us that we can live a victorious life if we do all according to the word of God and meditate on it day and night and if we do that we will make our way prosperous and we will have good success. This is not a promise it is a principle, this is why God has in his word stressed the importance of study, seeking, knocking, getting wisdom and receiving his word the son of God. Having heaven on earth is what God desires for us to have this is why I am putting some of my thoughts down because we have so long been watching the world live if you will, "Heaven on Earth", most Christians are waiting for the great wealth transfer and they have not understood that it took place two thousand years ago when Jesus took back what the Devil stool from Adam. We have the power and that power is our faith but power unused is like a battery in a drawer its potential energy waiting for someone to put it to work, we must make our faith be as kinetic energy, power that is always moving like niagra falls. Like with a picture we have to stop focusing on one part of it and begin to look at the whole picture which is Jesus died and suffered for our wholeness not just for being saved but salvation the whole of life and in the following chapters I'm going to do my best to unfold this salvation a bit at a time for you so lets begin and go possess our land in Jesus name Amen.

Chapter 1

The Call for a People

God in all of his wisdom knows all that has taken place in this world from the beginning to now and unto the end. When satan tricked Adam and stoled the power over this earth God did not sweat it nor did he stop Adam from eating the forbidded fruit and nor will he stop you from whatever vice you have or are engaging yourself in. God had a plan a remedy for mans fall to bring us back to him because man is to look to God as their source. So God said "I need a body", because God knew that man could not fix this situation they cause. So God call a man name Abram and told him that through you all the nations of the earth would be blessed. Regardless of what Abram could or could not do was of no significances to God because God would fight all the battles, open and closed all the doors and do all the things needed to be done through the faith of Abram.

Abram listened to God's words and faith came and Abram continued to hear God and Faith kept growing until Abram became Abramham a father of many nations and so a people is called and for forty two generations God dwelled with his call out ones through many events. As you look in the recorded writings of God's word we can see that Isreal has been watched over and kepted alive by God many times. When the people of God remembered the God of their fathers Abramham, Isaac and Jacob they cried out to him and God because of his promise to Abramham he anwsered to keep the promised seed alive. Today we that are under Grace have the same loving and kind God looking after us as did the children of Isreal but God is still waiting for us to answer the call and receive the promise as the seed of Abramham. What I mean is that we must remember who God is and that he is our source for victory on the earth. Like Isreal did in Egypt they remembered and called on God for help and if we make an effort to cry out to

God to answer his call on our life he will answer us. But we can't try and figure God out, faith is not looking for the way God is going to answer our particular problem remember faith don't look for what it suppose to already have, faith is the substances of things hopeful and the evidence of things not seen not the evidence I'm looking to see. We got to know God has already worked it out for our good, remember Gods plan in Genesis the results of his plan is shown in Revelations, we win but in order to win we must engage in the study of God's word and allow the Holy Spirit to reveal Jesus to us in other words God's written word revealed to us by revelation knowledge. Without revelation there is no manifestation we must understand what God is saying to us in his word because once you understand a thing no demon or devil can take what you know away. The only way revelation want help you if you reject it but that would be foolish, God is not calling fools to stay fools he's calling us to become the image of his dear son Jesus on the earth. Understanding the call of God is for all who would dare to answer no matter who you are black, white, brown, yellow, rich or poor whatever your status God is calling for whosoever. God is all knowing and if you believe that than receiving what God has called you to is easy because if you know he knows it all than waiting for the manifestation of his promise to the called ones is a breeze. The people God is calling is a people who are tired of just living, tired of just barely making it and tired of phoney friends but are ready to live abundantly a balanced life one where they can find and know the real them. To live this way is to totally trust God and not lean back on your thinking or understand on the way your life should go but in order not to fall back the people need a champion a deliverer so God call for a deliverer his name is Jesus. Now one thing that must be understood is that there is a time span between when you release your faith and believe God and when the manifestation of what you believe for appears. This time is not very comfortable I mean it can be down right nasty. Your faith is being tested, when the writer James said, "count it all joy when trouble comes, knowing that the testing of your faith workest patience" and it's going to be worked you can look at all the example of the scripture for instance, Job and Joseph. These men live's was just torn up from the floor up, Job lost all ten children his wife and his wealth but because he did not doubt God throw his religion away as most of us might do in his circumstances God restore everything he lost plus one of everything so Job got double for his trouble. Joseph, when you look at his life its like, my God, his own family turn against him some of his brothers wanted to kill him but you know they could not God had a plan for his life. So Joseph goes from pit to prison to the palace and it ended up those very people who threw him away had to come on bended knees. Is this a picture of Jesus, Jesus came unto his own and his own received him not but in Jesus' case he went from prison, to the pit and than to the palace where he sits at the right hand of God almighty and every knee must bow and tongue confess that Jesus is Lord. I wrote all that to express to you that when you endure like a good soldier there is a glorious reward waiting for you with your name on it on the other side. You can't know this except you are in the word of God and getting to know God's nature and you know that when you know Jesus in other words you have access to all of Heaven by the Holy Spirit. I want you to know you are going to be stretched to your limit and beyond but God is not going to let you snap because he loves you and wants you to succeed and he will help you to succeed only if you allow him to. How do you allow him to help you by obeying is commandments and in doing that you will prove to God that you love him because the only way you can prove to him you love is to obey him through his word the Bible. Oh my

God, when you reach the end of the trail and receive your breakthrough as Job and Joseph did the glory ole the glory the peace and the spirit of generosity that will come over you because you know all you need is God and anything else is nothing which makes it easier to be a blessing because whatever you give away God will give you double for your trouble, respond to God's call AMEN.

Chapter 2

The Devil Made My Bed and I Slept In It

There is a force that drives people from outside of them, there is a power that's imprisoned in an unlock jail on the inside of them. The answer to life is to allow the real you to come out of the unlock prison from inside of you. My point is stop allowing the outside seen forces to control the unseen you on the inside, your greatest you is still awaiting your call. The sadness about life is that we have no clue of who we are, and the proof is obvious by looking at junior high school students, at this age and younger we allow our children to be influenced by the media and television. Many times it is the parents that have the problem, unfulfilled dreams that had now become the dreams force on their children. Which creates a perpetual cycle that won't be broken until someone stands up and breaks the cycle. Let me be clear to say this is a form of child abuse howbeit a very mild and non-criminal case of abuse but nontheless can cause great damage. Some things that can occur from this form of abuse is resentment, resentment is a very powerful mild form of hate, in that it makes a person feel as if someone has violated their rights to live, (ie. Slavery) really when looking at parents that try to live life through their children or one of their children it looks like an obsession. Let me say this, not all situations like this is bad, some of our children really want to pursue the very same things that their parents were unable to pursue in the past for whatever reason. There are many cases like this but we as parents must be able to love our children regardless of the avenues they pursue, hard though it might be but we must consider the things we taught them and hope that they took it in. The Bible says that you must train up a child in the way they should go and when they are older it will not depart. That says a few things to me one is we must know our child and pay attention to their personalities as it develops. For instance, a child may have a desire to always help people whenever someone is hurting or injuried and asking questions regarding the hows, wheres, and whys of a persons sickness and if we training them up in the vain in which they demonstrate, exposing them to the many aspects of the medical field along with the other general studies they need to learn they begin at an early age the art of interdisciplinary learning a concept which opens many more doors of opportunity. This type of training if restricted causes a sense of narrow mindedness, leading to rebellion or a long time of unhappiness and resentment in the life of our children. We must teach our children at an early age how to reach inside of themselves and pull out the treasure on the inside of them. Now, getting a toddler to understand this natural process may not be easy but it is something that can be done. It is natural, for instance, children are not taught to lie they just do it, something on the inside of them say's to them self preservation don't make mommy mad at me and tell the truth that I did it, because I don't like mommy being angry with me. The trust children have for what is in them talking is extraordinary, and this is why God in his word say we must be like a child to enter into the Kingdom of Heaven, why? Because children are innocent the Bible says to the pure all things are pure but to the defiled and unbelieving nothing is pure. So when children are taught to be like God in their thinking, talking and living they can have a life of victorious living not free from trouble but freedom itself. Jesus said that we would have tribulation (ie. Trouble) in the world but be of good cheer for I have overcome this world, how did he do it, by being who he was and that was God. So as scripture says as Jesus was on the earth so are we which means we have the same power in us that was in Christ Jesus to bring us to an abundant life if we listen to who's inside of us, Jesus. I started off using children because they are the best way to show the perpetual effects of not guarding your heart and mind from outside influences that are not Godly, God said that he has given us everything pertaining to life and godliness, in other words that God-like-ness was already in you before you were born and every tool needed to succeed in life. God also said you have the mind of Christ not you can get or you must have but that you have it already. One more thing God said is that he has given you the power to create wealth so that he may establish his covenant in the earth, question, what is his covenant? What did he tell Adam? Simply to prosper, to build, to enlarge your self and to be an extension of God who is in Heaven on the earth. We are prisoners in the unlock prison inside of us which has no guards but us, we have been set free to live freely for years but we have allowed the enemy to (en-ner-my) enter us and make us hold ourselves captive not knowing we could have walk out at any time but we let ourselves be blinded from the truth by a liar. Let's release the treasures in us and allow the God-like-ness to flow freely out of us toward our fellow man, in Jesus name AMEN.

Chapter 3

Unity by Design

Unity by design is a process in which God pours himself out in three persons, the Father, the Son, and the Holy Spirit all acting in one purpose of mind and heart. By doing so, God has declared those who allow the one God in three persons to fill them up to walk in victory continuously. But there is only one problem that stops the continuous walk of victory and that is destiny's choice. This choice that God has set before us all is either to live life and Blessing or live death and cursing and the strange thing about it is God give us his advise, he tells us to choose life. Choose to live a victorious life daily, but we stop the flow of victories in our life because we can't walk in the design for unity God has scripted in his word because of what we see. Remember we the justified of God walk by faith not by sight and because we allow our eyes to decieve us into thinking what we see is more important than what can't be seen even though God says that what is made was not made by the things that do appear. In other words only the spirit can make or create and God is that Spirit. God's unity by design is setup by four key ingredients the first ingredient is Love, you cannot even consider a relationship with any thing or one without first adding love. The second ingredients is being of one mind, Paul said that we have the mind of Christ thus all who claim to be Christians have in fact the mind of Christ. The third ingredient is spiritual unity, we all have been filled with the Holy Spirit, once we ask Jesus into our life his spirit immediately comes and indwells within us. The fourth and final ingredient is to walk in one purpose, what is that purpose? That all should come to the knowledge of the saving grace of God through his son Jesus Christ, and this is done through the preached word of God by chosen men and women of God and for this purpose Jesus came into the world and through this purpose we have our mission in life or what I call Gods unity by design. Being united is a very powerful thing, when unity is created it brings success every time,there is nothing that a group that is united in one purpose can't do even in the face of adversity when the team stands together victory is always afoote. When you look at the account in the Bible when the tower of Babel was being built God said that these people are of one mind and there is nothing they can't do. We serve a God of unity we see that in the persons of God, God the Father, God the Son and God the Holy Spirit they are so united they are one. And this is the position Jesus prayed that the Church would be in, oneness like he and the Father are one. It's evident that the Church is far from unified with so many denominations setup because of disagreements. We have allowed the devil to trick us by believing we need to be the leader, I can do a better job. Let's be real about it, mostly every denomination start out of selfish ambitions a fallen out of some sort with the leader of an organization. And so now what most call unity in the Church is not it is simply uniformity, there is a difference in unity and uniformity. True unity is a matter of the heart. Uniformity is the result of pressures from outside your self. Since the believers are "in Christ," this ought to encourage them to work toward unity and love, not division and rivalry. In a gracious way, God is saying to the church, "Your disagreements reveal that there is a spiritual problem in your fellowship. And it isn't going to be solved by rules or threats; it's going to be solved when your hearts are right with Christ and with each other. Unity by design is a process just like any other in scripture that requires a choice to be made to walk in it; all the ingredients are automatically deposited within the believer at the new birth into christiandom. This means we all have the same love, Spirit, mind and oneness of purpose. But not all will allow these treasures to operate in their lives. Sometimes we as beleivers want to be the center of attention and we don't want to follow orders because we know we are Gods child too and he speaks to us just like this one or that one. When we do as Jesus did and humble ourselves and become as a bond servant not just a servant but a bond servant one who as Jesus did will cover a multitude of sins for a brother in other word not revealing the sin but forgiving and restoring one back to Christ. Having the mindset to count up the cost of your own salvation and then comforting another person with the same comfort where with Jesus comforted you. Although Jesus is God he did not demonstrate to the world his equality with God he emptied himself so that we could be full, full of what? Jesus's joy, peace his love and God's Spirit and glory. To choose not to walk in Gods unity by design is a tragedy of justice because what you give up is Gods best, not just for you but for the one's who could come to God through you. If Jesus in the garden had chosen to not stay in the unity of fellowship with God could you imagine what the people in the Church would be like, some of us are terrible now how would we be without Jesus' sacrifice. Jesus' sacrifice granted him the high place in God he is exalted, Jesus is our example and if we follow his example and become a servant to our brothers and sisters and stop trying to be their lord, God said that "Whoever exalts himself shall be made low, and whoever humbles himself shall be exalted. Not by man but by God, unity by design is that which makes the statement by Jesus to his diciples true, upon this rock I shall build my Church and the gates of hell shall not prevail against it. A house divide can not stand and a double minded person is unstable in all their ways let not that person, what person? The person who has the mind of Christ but decides not to walk in the fullness of it but instead decided to use some of the world's way of thinking to doing things. If you don't live the way God said you can't expect to receive anything from him. When we do it Gods way he will bring peace in our life, unity by design, when making that choice to surrender to God you will see how good he is, thank God and AMEN.

Chapter 4

A Prayer for God's Pardon for Self

Sometimes we forget about why we need God and his forgiveness through his son Jesus, and how we came to get it. We need it simply because we treat people the way we don't want to be treated, whether saved or not and it is not because we are not sincere in our walk with God, it's because we get so caught up in being saved we never take the time to learn how to live save. We've accepted Christ but continued to live like a sinner with Christian tendencies, until we have a Nathan experience that is, being confronted with the truth about ourselves Psalms 51 has no bearing in our lives. Until that happens God has to disapprove of some things in our lives, that goes for me, you, the Ushers, choir, Deacons, Ministers, Pastors especially, trustees, pew members everybody. Christians seem to think just because they are saved they can excuse their behavior of how they treat people. We throw so many people away because they have done something not in line with the word of God and I have found that the very thing that person did is the same thing the leader of the throw away mob did earlier in their short life. They never think about the fact that this person got caught during their time of leadership because they did the same thing early in their life and God wanted to use them to lead a sinner or a Christian who according to the word God needs restoring back to right standing. To restore such a one in love and with the same grace, mercy and comfort given to them by God because all have sinned and fallen short of the glory of God. We have to forget about the bling bling ghetto mentalility in the pulpit, I got to drive the best cars live in the best house and dress the best. What we have taught people in the church and outside is that we are like pimps. I know some Pastors are not going to like this but if you look at the comparisons for example: a pimp start off treating the prospective whore like a queen getting her to really like him and to believe he has her best interest at heart. Once the pimp know he got her where he wants her he tells her to help with some money because he is a little short on cash and because she loves him she says of course I'll help you, you been so good to me what do you need me to do, you know the rest. Now there are some Pastors not unlike a pimp and some may not believe they are but there actions speak louder than words. A visitor come to visit they treat them with the red carpet treatment especially if the person is a non-churched person with a significant job. They join and if they fall into place, in other words don't think for themselves, then the Pastor begins to tell them his plan to help the community clean up the urban plight or surburban and because the Pastor knows that this is dear to the persons heart he let's them know how much money is needed and you know the rest. Now let me say this if you are and your Pastor is a true Christian man or woman then don't get angry about what is being written but if you are angry then it's you or your pastor. See we got pimps driving brand new expensive car and the prostitutes are on the bus and living in substandard housing. There are Pastors driving expensive cars and their parishioners are on the bus and living in substandard housing. Now is there something wrong with pastors living in good homes and driving new cars absolutely not, pastors must show there people how by natural ways and not just tell them to have faith sow seeds and you can have what I have. Show them how to start a business, invest etc. People don't bring their hard earned money to the church so that the Pastor can live a hip hop celebrity lifestyle. What breaks my heart is the community is dying right in front of there eyes and all they ask is for more money the first fruits the tithe your offering. Millions of dollar budgets for TV to reach millions not to save them but to offer products and asks for seed offerings not all that are on TV is like this there are many men of God on TV that are for real. I was a business student in college and took marketing and I know the numbers, TV is not only for reaching people for salvation it is for the money. Why would you go on TV when the community around the church needs evangelizing it not because their not out there it because some are scared of the people and I mean some black preacher are afraid of black people. I don't see the Jesus in the Bible in the church much any more it's not love, they make it seem like God is not God. Some Preachers are very nasty when they challenge people to give, when will we follow Christ, Jesus was never unkind. A lot of Pastors have a pharisee mentality they have a form of godliness and deny the power of God because the money is their power. They say the Bible talk about money more than anything but does that take presecdant over salvation, forgiveness of sin, loving your neighbor or God, no. The Bible also talks about babies being killed a lot in it but we don't go randomly killing babies that are already born. The reality of the Bible is reconciliation God building a bridge between himself and man to restore the relationship between God and man through the bridge Jesus Christ. The church is so messed up that Pastors are getting divorce both the wife and the husband are Pastors and divorce because of irreconcilible differences and that is shameful because what it simply proves is that the anointing is not the burden removing yoke destroying power of God. At least only when it concerns you those who listen to the Preacher not the Preachers, where is your faith Preacher God can do any thing but fail, but people can fail, certainly Pastors and Preachers can. I can really see why people don't like the Church because it is fill with some of the most hypocritical people and liars in the world. The Church teaches act like Jesus who hung out with the sinners and publicans but the church can turn there backs on a man who help and lead the way for many black Preacher as well as some whites to mainstream evangelism, Carlton Pearson, all because he wanted inclusion for whoever wanted to come to hear Gods word. Would these people be consider sinners that he wanted to include the very same people Jesus came down to save, society as a whole will throw you away if they think you are guilty, look at OJ Simpson found innocent by a jury of his community but yet just because people believe he is guilty but don't really know for sure they treat him bad and took everything he owned. This is just like a non-believer's point of view about God, it is proven in nature and space and in many other ways that there is a God but yet more don't believe than believe and does that stop God from demonstrating his love to all mankind, the answer is no, than what the hell is wrong with the church, start loving everybody just like your God or is your god the money you collect on Sunday.

Chapter 5

Why Do Bad Things Happen To Good People?

Can we add anything to ourselves? Can we make ourselves taller, skin lighter, or darker? If we are bald can we cause our hair to grow, make our nose shrink, lips thicker the answer to these questions is a resounding NO! We can't, although God has given us a great deal of freedom and creativity and free will we are still subjective to some uncontrollable events in life. Whether good or bad these uncontrolled events happen, they just happen to you and me, to Christian and sinners. But why, is it because of life itself or do we individually cause or create these uncontrolled events to occur in our own lives, why is it that a honor student gets involved with someone going nowhere and that someone takes them exactly nowhere. Take the pyramid scheme, how many time have you or someone you know gotten caught-up in a get rich quick thing and lost hundred of dollars, I could go on forever with examples but I believe you follow me on this. Now the question is who is really in control of your life? So many of us have said God is in control of our life and that is true to a point, you submit and yield your will to him. God has given us dominion, and a free will, which gives us control, God said I set before you blessing and cursing life and death God wants us to choose life and blessing not death but the key word here is choose, who's choice is it? Ours, not Gods, we can't choose our beginning but we do have a choice of how our life can finish. This is why I ask the question why do bad things happen to good people? I will do my best to explore this question and others as they arise enjoy.

"Purpose"

Bad things happen to good people because good people sow bad seeds and I know that is an oxymoron but yes, good people because of spiritual blindness and under develop study habits and uncontrolled carnal thoughts sow bad seeds. Let's look at a biblical example; Job is a prime example of a good person who knew God. Job because of his fears opened the door to allow the devil to cause the destruction of his children and wealth and even afflictions to his own physical body. Job recovered all he had lost and more only because he trusted God in his suffering and did not forget God and he learned the error of his ways, thoughts and words, for he said at the end that the very thing that he feared had come upon him, God did not give us the spirit of fear but of love and peace and a sound mind. Bad things happen to good people to move them into their purpose in life not only to move them but also to prepare them for that purpose. People spend much time and money trying to figure out what is the purpose for their life, everyone has a purpose or a reason for birth and unfortunately not everyone fulfills their purpose, on purpose. A person's purpose is not always a good thing some people's purpose are to be an instrument of destruction and terror. Some of the key changes in the lives of people occur during or because of tragedy, not individuals only but also families, nations, and the world. One of the most horrific purposes a person has had was to suffer and die at the hand of men so that all mankind could live and the affects of his purpose is still affecting mankind today and that person is our Lord and Savior Jesus Christ. What are you passionate about what do you love doing will you do it for free? Finding your purpose is as easy as asking, seeking, and knocking but it is to whom you are asking, seeking, and whose door you're knocking on. If it is man than you want find your purpose it has to be the creator of all thing and that is JESUS. Without purpose we will find ourselves falling into many pitfalls in life some we caused our self and others because of following someone who knows his purpose or someone who has no clue of what their purpose is. Examine your life and see if you are consistently running into problems and primarily the same kind of problem and if you are consider seeking the kingdom of God first and prove God through doing his word.

"Right Words"

Words are more than just sounds that travel from a person's mouth to someone's ears. Words are thoughts spoken, and these words frame our very existence from the time we are able to speak we begin to frame our future. If we could in detail look back in our past we would see that everything that has occurred in our lives were framed by the thoughts and words we have spoken. Just as in the book of Hebrews the Bible says, "The world was framed by the words of GOD" because we are made in the image and likeness of GOD we to can frame our world because our words are spirit and they are life. I guess we start out in life where our family is when we are born and as we grow we learn life words and death words and somewhere along our life path we must learn to use right words to frame the kind of life GOD has purposed for us. What I mean is we hear words and some times these words stick with us for life, word like your lazy, or stupid, and one we all say a lot the word crazy. Most of the times these words are said to us by people we believe know what they are talking about or we love like Mom, Dad, grandparents, teachers, and others we look up to. What we as individuals have to learn are to say encouraging word or words that edify the ones hearing them including your self. Just one word can destroy a life, that life will speak death into another life and a continual cycle has begun. Speaking right words is so very important to the development of life the psalmist wrote that "the tongue is the pen of a ready writer". What he is saying is that when we speak every word is being recorded and immediately our words are being carried out. Ultimately our words will return to us accomplishing whatever we said. Here is another area that contributes to the reason why bad things happen to good people and another answer is we speak words of negative, sickness, craziness, loneliness, poverty, and some people even speak death in their life. We often say no one really wants bad things to happen to them but when we examine the evidence of people's life we more often than not find out that the beginning of the bad thing started in their mind and eventually came out of their mouth which triggered that which followed, God have mercy AMEN.

Chapter 6

Dying For a Man

Have you ever told some one that you did not want to do something when you really did? That is denial, or lying to yourself not giving yourself an opportunity to try something new that can maybe enhance yours or someones life you love. Denial for our purpose mean: a psychological/mental defense mechanism in which confrontation with a personal problem or with reality is avoided by denying the existence of the problem or reality. Often young women find themselves in situations where they feel that they need a man but they never take the time to understand the type of man that can meet their personal and emotional needs. More often than not, young women end up in a bad relationship which than leads to abuse and ultimately denial which is the first line of defense women use to combat their false realities. That false reality is that the man loves them, the very first thing the guy does is to get her to believe he loves her and believe in him and his dream or lack of a dream and that his so called dream includes her . After he convinces her of that he knows she's sprung. Now he goes into I need, can I use, loan me this amount, the training mode. All while he is doing this training he loves on her more than she has ever been loved on in her life and now her family can't say anything wrong about him this puts him in a position of I can do no wrong. This is when some verbal abuse starts to happen because a dependency is now beginning to form between the both of them first her's is needing his loving touch in the form of sex mostly and for him is needing any and every thing she has that helps him live and feel important. Men with daughters we must love our girls and talk to them more to let them know that they are special so that when these young guys try to run game they won't be the ones who get played. For the girls and women who are dealing with denial regarding these so called men that you are dealing with, you have to know that putting on blind folds yourself is like committing suicide because a lot of you say to your family and friend concerned about you that I know he is that but he has good qualities you don't see and anyway I love him. True love from a real man is such that his life needs and lifes pleasures come second to yours and the family. Unfortunately many Christian women go through this more often than women who don't know God because they are believing for a husband and can't wait for God to bring their husband, they end up with a bum, a user or someone who fakes being a christian just to get them because like Marvin Gaye said, "I need a sanctified women" why because they will take care of them and he knows where they are, at Church. All while he is doing any and everything he wants while she's in Church service, we all, men and women need to develop a more disiplined life in how we approach studing and appling the word of God to our individual lives because we are destroying ourselves, a lack of knowledge causes people to be destroyed stop the stupidity. Dying for a mans touch, why can't you die for a touch from God, by the act of the Holy Spirit your God kind of man will show up in your life right on time but you got to trust God to do it in his time not yours, remember if you can believe all things are possible to them who continue to believe God.

Chapter 7

The Call for a Deliverer, Don't Move Until God Say Move

Let's go back to the cry of the Hebrew slaves in Egypt, they cry out to God for help and God prepared for them a deliverer, lets look back. During the time of Moses birth the king of Egypt ordered that the male child two years and under be killed in every Hebrew home and at that time Moses was born. God used Moses mother, gave her wisdom to preserve Moses and put him in a basket so that the daughter of the King would find him and raise him as her own son and Marion Moses sister follow the basket and told the Princess that her mother could nurse him for her and so she agreed. Moses was raised in all the glory as an Egyptian the grandson of the King of Egypt. One day Moses was out riding and saw a taskmaster beating a Hebrew slave trying to be a deliverer before his time and ended up killing the taskmaster and buried him and the Hebrews saw this. Later on he saw two Hebrews fighting and Moses tried to be a deliverer before his time and said to them why are you fight your brother? They mocked him and said who are you to talk when you killed another Egyptian. After that Moses became a fugative and stayed away from Egypt for forty years until it was time for him to deliver God's people by the hand of God and not his. Sometimes we move before God tells us to we have the gift in us to do what it is God would have us do and we jump the gun and mess things all up but when its our time and we wait on God we have all of Heaven backing us as we follow the direction of the Holy Spirit. The call of God is a call that resounds, as Niagra Falls continues to fall and as I write God is waiting for those to whom he is calling to answer. The call will take them that answer through a gambit of ups and downs and changes and turn arounds. Through it all God will be right there to strengthen all by his Grace.

Thank you for taking the time to read what I believe the Lord has given me to write God Bless you all and keep you until the day of Jesus' return. AMEN

Kevin B. Thomas is an associate minister at Mt. Zion Missionary Baptist Church located in the city of Ecorse, Michigan. Kevin has attended Heritage College and Seminary and plan to continue his education. The central theme of his message is helping Christian's find and discover their hidden potential, and teaching that to reach your potential in Christ there are times of testing coming. Teaching also keys to help endure through the test, which are the love of God, the Spirit of God, and the Word of God and the biggest key is giving God's love away to others. Kevin has been married to his wife Deanna for twenty years and has two children, Kevin II and Nicole.